W9-AEJ-124

Handbook for Today's Catholic Family

A REDEMPTORIST PASTORAL PUBLICATION

Liguori
ONE LIGUORI DRIVE
LIGUORI MO 63057-9999

Imprimi Potest:
Thomas D. Picton, C.Ss.R.
Provincial, Denver Province
The Redemptorists

Imprimatur:
Most Reverend Robert J. Hermann
Auxiliary Bishop, Archdiocese of St. Louis

Liguori Publications, a nonprofit corporation, is an apostolate of the Redemptorists. To learn more about the Redemptorists, visit Redemptorists.com.

To order, call 800-325-9521.
www.liguori.org

CONTENTS

INTRODUCTION

Jewish oral tradition holds that a rabbi who lived in Kraków dreamed three times that an angel told him to go to Livovna. "In front of the palace there, near a bridge," the angel said, "you will learn where a treasure is hidden."

The rabbi went to Livovna. When he arrived at the palace, he found a sentinel near the bridge, so he told him the dream. The sentinel replied, "I, too, have had a dream. The angel told me to go to a rabbi's house in Kraków, where a treasure is buried in front of the fireplace." Hearing this, the rabbi returned home and dug in front of his fireplace. There he found the treasure.

As a *family*, you have a treasure that surpasses all human expectations. That treasure is waiting to be discovered in your own home.

As a *Catholic*, you possess a family treasure that can transform your life together into an experience of peace and joy. That treasure is also waiting to be discovered in your own home.

You are the rabbi, and this booklet is the sentinel. The sentinel's message is this: *The kingdom of God is among you.*

1

YOU ARE CALLED TO DISCOVER THE KINGDOM

(CCC* 541–555; 2232–2233)

Paradise Lost

Young children have little trouble believing in a heavenly kingdom where life ever after is filled with family, friends, and endless ice cream sundaes. A child will spend hours imagining a fantasy world that reflects current fiction or film images in which happiness abounds. The joy found in such imaginative play disappears gradually as the child grows into adolescence; it sometimes disappears entirely in adulthood, when many people lose the ability to focus on a heavenly kingdom.

Once we enter the world of adult and family responsibilities, life becomes work, work, work. It's a rat race we don't especially like but which we cannot stop. Life becomes the joyless burden of Adam and Eve banished from Paradise.

When most of us were children, we had the normal cares children have. But for most of us, life was an almost-carefree existence, a dwelling in the fantasy land of an eternal now. As

---

*Catechism of the Catholic Church

we reached school age, we developed the desire to grow up, but even the adulthood we envisioned was a fantasy. We hoped to be movie stars or sports celebrities and live happily ever after.

Now here we are in adulthood, the long middle stage between our first and second childhoods. Few of us are movie stars or sports celebrities. We work at raising a family, adjusting to change, and finding peace of mind amid life's daily struggles.

For many people, the search for peace of mind and a sense of joy seems like an uphill climb. We want to break down artificial barriers and be ourselves. We want to be real with each other. We want, deep down, to believe that life is unbelievably good and that it never ends. We want to be responsible adults, but we also want to live life with the "vision splendid" our children and grandchildren possess.

Is there a way to regain that vision?

The Vision Regained

In his first letter to Corinth, Paul wrote, "When I became an adult, I put an end to childish ways" (13:11). He was addressing a group of adults trying to upstage each other by claiming they had various spiritual gifts (12—14). These Christians were so busy with their petty scheming and rivalries that they lost sight of their original vision. They had fallen into the trap of playing games with each other, a characteristic of the adult world. Paul was telling them all this adult game-playing is really childish.

The opposite of childishness is the radically mature vision Jesus revealed. He said, "Change and become like children" (Matthew 18:3). This strange advice sounds foolish by our adult standards. That's the point. It cuts through all the adult foolishness that makes us unhappy. Very simply, in Paul's words, "God's foolishness is wiser than human wisdom" (1 Corinthians 1:25).

God's foolishness knows what adult wisdom does not know:

We cannot make ourselves happy. What the wise child in us wants is attainable—but we can attain it only by entering the world of Gospel simplicity. Saint Thérèse of Lisieux found great joy in the humility of following the ways of a child in her relationship with God: "to expect everything from the goodness of God, exactly as a little child expects everything from his father" (*Thérèse of Lisieux: In My Own Words,* Liguori Publications, 2005). Such a humble heart expects and requires only love, not earthly glory or wealth, "not even the glory of Heaven—that belongs by right to my brothers the Angels and Saints, and my own glory will be the radiance that streams from the queenly brow of my Mother, the Church" (*The Autobiography of St. Thérèse of Lisieux With Additional Writings and Sayings of St. Thérèse*, Project Gutenberg, 2005).

We can become like that. We can experience what Saint Paul called "the freedom of the glory of the children of God" (Romans 8:21).

The proposal is utterly serious: *Change.* Become like children. Study the attitudes that set them apart from the world of adult wisdom. Pick a child you know whose life embodies the view of life you want to regain. You certainly know such a child. In fact, she or he may very well live with you.

Study the child. Briefly list her or his characteristics—things like trust, wonder, innocence, joy. Get inside the child's mind and explore where these attitudes come from. Ask yourself why he or she feels this way. Ask yourself whether he or she is foolish or whether this is the way life really is—the way it can be for you.

Children know what Jesus means by *blessed* in chapter 5 of Matthew. They know what Paul means by *joy* in his letter to the Philippians. In the world of most children, life is unbelievably good and never ends. That world is exactly what Jesus was talking about when he spoke of the kingdom.

That world can be your world. You can see your own life in a new light. You can experience "the vision splendid" within your own home. But to regain that vision, you must take Jesus with utter seriousness. He was speaking to *adults* when he said, "Change and become like children."

The Family of the Kingdom

Jesus of Nazareth, the traveling preacher, had no property, no children, no steady job. You might not think such a person would be a great family man. But he was exactly that. The difference was this: Everybody was family who wanted to belong.

It all stemmed from the way Jesus saw reality. To him, home was the presence of God. He was aware of God the way you are aware of yourself—always and everywhere. In those days it was considered irreverent even to speak the name of God in public. The name was too sacred. But Jesus went much further than *saying* God's name; he called God *Abba*—"beloved father." His relationship with God was so deep and natural it was catching. Everyone he influenced was drawn into it. Even today, people still talk to God in Jesus' daring terms: we call God our *Father.*

Jesus was a rabbi, a religious teacher. But because of the way he saw reality, he was not like other rabbis. Jesus' awareness was that the Father is preparing a great banquet for us in his kingdom. The strange thing about this banquet is its time and place. The time of the banquet is now; Jesus was constantly telling people the banquet has begun. And the place for the banquet isn't somewhere else. It's right here: Jesus insisted that "the kingdom of God is among you" (Luke 17:21). This awareness was so deep and radical that people still don't grasp it very well. The banquet in the kingdom is here and now? What does that mean?

John the Baptizer was a contemporary of Jesus', a visionary holy man if ever there was one. John was incredibly strict with himself. His clothing was made of camel hair, and his food was locusts and wild honey. John told people that the kingdom is at hand and urged them to repent.

Jesus said something similar, but his awareness of God was vastly different from John's. In Jesus' awareness the banquet had already begun; this was no time for strict fasting. So Jesus made the rounds, eating and drinking with all kinds of people, respectable or otherwise. The contrast between Jesus and John was so sharp that a saying about it appears in the Gospel: "For John came neither eating nor drinking, and they say, 'He has a demon'; the Son of Man came eating and drinking, and they say, 'Look, a glutton and a drunkard'" (Matthew 11:18–19). Jesus was neither a glutton nor a drunkard, but he was very serious about the banquet. The time is now, he would say. The kingdom is in our midst, and the banquet has already begun.

The Kingdom Here and Now

No one can tell us what the banquet really is. It can't be explained; it can only be discovered. But we do know this: God is involved in it. God is our beloved Father, and you are his beloved family. Your family is God's family, whether led by two parents, a single father or single mother, a grandparent, or stepparent. Every person in your family, respectable or otherwise, has a place in the kingdom.

The kingdom image long ago conjured up a benevolent king and queen with heir-apparent prince and beautiful princess. In this twenty-first century, our family kingdoms look less and less like this storybook image; their realities reflect the current statistics of single-parent homes and families blended as much by diversity as by economics. Regardless of a family's makeup, the Catholic Church upholds its sacred nature and values the family as a "community of faith, hope, and charity; it assumes singular importance in the Church, as is evident in the New Testament" (*CCC* 2204).

No one can define the kingdom. It has no boundaries of time or place. But this much is known: for you, it is here and now in your family. The nature of the kingdom is such that you experience it through others—especially those who mean the most to you. For you, the banquet takes place in your family, or it does not take place at all.

The kingdom is not something you can make happen. Only God can do that. It lies in your future with God. The kingdom appears in your midst to lead you forward into that future. You and your family are pilgrims traveling to a kingdom not of this world.

The banquet you are called to is not literally a meal. As Paul wrote, "For the kingdom of God is not food and drink but righteousness and peace and joy in the Holy Spirit" (Romans 14:17). You cannot create this peace and joy. But you *can* discover it and experience it in your spouse, your parents, your children, your brothers, and your sisters. In the happiness you share with one another, you recognize that the peace and joy of the banquet are a reality you actually experience. Whenever you forgive each other or do something to heal a wound, God is at work within you. When you look at each other and realize the Father is calling this person to communion with himself, the kingdom is in your midst.

The person who called us to the kingdom is very family-minded. To him, his Father means everything. Bringing people together to experience the peace and joy of the Holy Spirit was the whole point of his life. His family is everybody who wants to belong to it, and his invitation to the banquet is especially for you. You must believe that—otherwise, it doesn't mean much to say, "the kingdom of God is among you" (Luke 17:21).

How to Use This Handbook

The "Points for Reflection and Dialogue" at the end of each chapter will enable you and your family to become closer and happier—more Christian, more Catholic.

Use these questions to write your own book. It might take weeks, even months, but if you commit to the project and follow it to the end, you'll create a family treasure. More suggestions:

- **Write the book as a family.** Have everyone who can write answer the questions on paper. Children who cannot write can draw. Some may want to write *and* draw. Then share your answers. Take turns talking, and listen carefully. Never argue; instead, try to understand each person's feelings and experiences. Do everything to make each session as enjoyable as possible. Eat and drink together: the kingdom of God is among you.
- **Have one family session per week.** Take one chapter at a time or stay with the same chapter over two or three sessions until you've covered all the questions.
- **Use only the questions everyone can relate to.** Some of the questions aren't for everyone. The chapters about marriage are beyond the experience of children. Simplify questions for younger members or make up your own questions.
- **Save all the papers you write and draw on.** Collect them, date them, and put them into a special family scrapbook. If you write this book a second time, you'll want to see your writings from the first time. But even if you never rewrite this book, it will be an heirloom that reveals your family's hearts and souls to your children's children.

Points for Reflection and Dialogue

1. My most beautiful memory from early childhood is... (describe as fully as possible).
2. The most kingdomlike quality each member of our family possesses is... (write each person's name and kingdomlike quality).
3. The characteristic of our family that means the most to me is... (describe how you feel and how different your life would be without this reality).
4. The last time I experienced the peace and joy of God's kingdom here at home was when... (describe what happened and how you felt about it).
5. When I think about God's calling each member of this family to communion with himself, I feel...
6. When I think about the kingdom of God being right here in our family, I realize that...

2

YOU ARE CALLED TO BE
THE BODY OF JESUS CHRIST

(*CCC* 764–766)

Saint Paul's Damascus Experience

An event that has profoundly shaped your view of life is recorded in chapters 9, 22, and 26 of Acts of the Apostles, in which a man named Saul of Tarsus was heading north on the road from Jerusalem to Damascus. His mission was to capture some members of the Way, a strange offshoot of Judaism that worshiped a dead Jew named Jesus of Nazareth. As Saul neared Damascus, there was a flash of light. Saul heard a voice say, "'Saul, Saul, why do you persecute me?' [Saul] asked, 'Who are you, Lord?' The reply came, 'I am Jesus, whom you are persecuting.'"

Blinded by the experience, Saul was led by the hand into Damascus to the home of a member of the Way. For three days Saul remained sightless, neither eating nor drinking. When Ananias, called by God to visit this blind man, laid his hands on Saul's head, "something like scales fell from his eyes" (Acts 9:18). He could see. Saul was then baptized on the spot. After that he ate some food and started regaining his strength.

The rest is history. Saul (also known as Paul, Acts 13:9) went on to preach, write, travel, do time in countless jails, and survive countless beatings. By the end of his life, Paul had spread the Way throughout the Near East.

All Paul ever said or did as an apostle flowed from that experience. During his three days of blindness, and for the rest of his life, that voice echoed in his mind: "I am Jesus, whom you are persecuting." These people he had captured and imprisoned—in some way, they *were* Jesus. That was the staggering truth contained in the revelation "Why do you persecute me?"

But that was not all. If Jesus was somehow one with his followers, it meant he was not dead but alive—alive in them and everywhere else. He could break into a person's life anytime, anywhere—for example, on a dirt road outside Damascus. He lives. *He lives!*

You, Too, Are Called to Damascus

In 1964, a year after his election to the papacy, Pope Paul VI wrote an encyclical called *Ecclesiam Suam* in which he quoted the fifth-century words of Saint Augustine, who was echoing the Damascus experience of Paul. The Scripture passage says, "For just as the body is one and has many members, and all the members of the body, though many, are one body, so it is with Christ....Now you are the body of Christ and individually members of it" (1 Corinthians 12:12–27).

This echo cuts through the sound and fury arising from change in the Church. It takes us past the surface to the very heart of Christianity: Jesus lives. We are his body. The time to rejoice is now.

This echo also calls you to change any attitude standing between you and the body. For example:

- **Do unpleasant memories of the Church in the past keep you away from the Church in the present?** If so, consider this: Jesus lives now in his body, the Church. The Church is now, not in the past.
- **Do teachings or rules or practices in the Church keep you from loving the Church itself?** If so, consider this: we—not things and practices—are the body of Jesus. To be a whole body, we need you. Don't let *things* keep you from us.
- **Do feelings against anyone keep you from living an active life in the body of Jesus?** If so, consider this: That person is not the whole Christ. Do your best to reconcile with that person, but do not reject the body of Christ because of one member.
- **Do teachings on divorce or annulment cause you to feel unwelcome within the body of Christ?** Your current situation may cause shame or a sense of inadequacy and imperfection in light of the traditions upheld by the Church. Don't let confusion, anger, or hopelessness keep you from understanding that, even in your brokenness, you are an important member in the Church.

Your Own Family Is the Body of Christ

In the Dogmatic Constitution on Divine Revelation (*Dei Verbum*), Pope Paul VI states that Church tradition *develops*, that "there is a growth in insight into the realities and words that are being passed on" (8).

A good case of such growth is the Pope's view that the family is "what might be regarded as the domestic Church" (Dogmatic Constitution on the Church [*Lumen Gentium*], 11).

After Vatican II, Pope Paul VI returned again and again to this point of the family as Church in his speeches. In his 1975 apostolic exhortation Evangelization in the Modern World (*Evan-*

gelii Nuntiandi), Pope Paul wrote that the family "has rightly been called the *domestic* church.…[I]n every Christian family the various features and characteristics of the universal Church should be found" (71).

That ray of light puts your family, traditional in its makeup or not, in a whole new perspective. It says that as Church,

- your family is the visible Body of Jesus Christ; and
- your family is the "universal sacrament of salvation," revealing God's incredible love inside your family and out.

Your Family As Church

With this new development in Church tradition, the nature of Christianity itself has become more clear. Just when you may have settled into thinking that *Church* meant bishops, priests, and religious, the word comes through that *Church* means your family. *The family has always been Church.* You have a calling to live with such undisguised joy that people would say, "I want to belong to that. Look how they love one another."

The Church is a family, and your flesh-and-blood family is Church. Your family is not perfect. But then, when was the Church *ever* perfect? Your family has problems. But do they match the problems of the people in Paul's first letter to the Corinthians, whom he refers to throughout as "the saints"?

Perfection is not the point. Current statistics remind us that the family unit is a reflection of the social identities of its culture. The number of children living in single-family homes is increasing, and nearly seventy percent of American youth live in nontraditional families. But regardless of the statistics, we are called as family to do our best to

- help each other believe the Good News even though it's so good it's hard to believe;
- see Jesus in each other;
- dare to talk to God as *Abba*, the Father who has made your family *his* family; and
- realize more and more that your family is *his* body, that whatever happens to one of you happens to *him*.

Your oneness with Jesus is rooted in your baptism, a reality that takes you into the heart of mystery. For example, "Do you not know that all of us who have been baptized into Christ Jesus were baptized into his death?" (Romans 6:3).

This oneness you share with his death through baptism makes you one with him in his new, unending life. Through baptism, "all of you are one in Christ Jesus" (Galatians 3:28). This reality deserves to be celebrated—this is something you can do on the anniversary of each family member's baptism. This basic oneness is also something to keep very clearly in mind if your family members are baptized Christians but not members of the Catholic Church.

In some mysterious way, your family is one with Jesus. Through your family, he lives and invites people to the banquet. He is doing it through you, and he will keep doing it until finally one day—as Saint Augustine wrote—"there will be one Christ, loving himself." (From *Love and Saint Augustine* by Hannah Arendt, University of Chicago Press, 1998).

Points for Reflection and Dialogue

1. When I think of Jesus as really *living*, the main thought that comes to me is…
2. The thing I like most about the Church today is…
3. The main way I can help our family realize what great faith we already have is…
4. The one Catholic I know who helps me more than anyone to be closer to God is…
5. When I realize that to love or hurt my fellow Catholics is to love or hurt Jesus' body and Jesus himself, I want to…
6. When I think about our family as called to reveal God's love at home and to other people, the main thought that comes to me is…
7. When I think that whatever happens to any member of our family happens to Jesus, the feeling I have is…
8. We want to deepen our family oneness in Jesus by celebrating the anniversaries of our baptisms. These dates are… (list dates).

3

SPOUSES ARE CALLED TO COMMUNICATE

(*CCC* 2201–2203)

Communication Is the Heart of Marriage

The musical *Fiddler on the Roof* is set in a Jewish village in Russia in 1905. Tevye the milkman has been married to Golde for twenty-five years. Their marriage was arranged by a matchmaker. As Tevye watches his daughters bypass the matchmaker tradition and marry for love, he starts wondering about Golde's feelings for him. When he asks whether she loves him, Golde recounts the hard life she has shared with him and concludes that she does indeed love him. They realize that, although saying the words aloud won't make a real difference in their lives, it still feels good to hear it.

And it *does* feel good to hear it. But it's more than just a good feeling, for the words *I love you* hide even more than they reveal. If you can say those words to your spouse, you can reach back to where they came from and reveal much more. And what you find yourself revealing can stop you in your tracks. Using various approaches, many thousands of couples have actually done this. They have dipped into their consciousness past all the memories, and have come up with deep, personal feelings they hardly suspected were alive in their hearts:

- "It's funny how you can live with someone for so many years and not realize how much you love him. I love you so much I can't believe it."
- "I've always been so independent and work-oriented, but what I've really wanted all these years is your love."
- "I never realized how much you mean to me. If you died, I don't know how I could go on living."

These are not words made up by songwriters. They're the deep-down realizations of middle-aged and older couples. They are *the real thing.*

This kind of communication is the heart of your marriage, because it gives you an experience of oneness that draws you even closer. It's an act of love that creates deeper love.

Verbal communication means talking on the same wavelength, being tuned in to each other. It's more than conversation, more than discussion. It's the opposite of debate, in which you try to drive home points and win. It's your listening to each other, really paying attention to each other's here-and-now *feelings* even more than to the words. It's your revealing of self to each other, especially your deep sense of oneness with each other.

In even the closest of marriages, negative feelings crop up between spouses. Given the complexity of personalities and the strains under which people live, conflict and stress are inevitable. For example, if both of you have been coping with chaos at opposite ends of town, it's not easy to tune in to each other when you meet at the end of the day. Many couples cope with negative feelings by fighting and then lapsing into silence. Others shut each other out from the start by going into a trance with a newspaper, television, or some form of work.

The way to avoid such noncommunication is to choose firmly and deliberately to communicate. Verbal communication, or dialogue, cuts through negative feelings and draws two people together.

Pope Paul's Guidelines for Dialogue

These guidelines for dialogue Pope Paul VI offered in his encyclical letter *Ecclesiam Suam* fit many situations, including dialogue between spouses:

BE CLEAR

Clarity before all else;...what is said should be intelligible (81.1).

An important point in this regard is preparation. You cannot abruptly say "Let's talk" and expect instant dialogue. If you want to get down to real sharing, agree on a time when everything will be calm and quiet. If you spring a dialogue on your partner and launch into something delicate, you are inviting tongue-tied confusion. Give each other time to ask, "Why do I want to talk?" If you want to talk to discuss or persuade, that's one thing. If you want to talk to get on the same wavelength and deepen your sense of oneness, that's something else. If you want a true dialogue, take aim. Aim to express yourself clearly and specifically, avoiding general-statement words like "always" and "never." Aim to listen and experience each other as clearly as possible.

BE MEEK

Dialogue must be accompanied by that meekness which
Christ bade us learn from Himself: "Learn from me; for
I am gentle and humble in heart, and you will find rest
for your souls" (81.2; Matthew 11:29).

Christ is neither boastful nor resentful in conversation with others, even with those who wish him harm. Sometimes your feelings may urge you to "come out fighting." *Don't do it.* If you have a complaint with some third party, don't take it out on your spouse. If you have a complaint with your spouse, that's a different case; your instinct then is to change your spouse's attitude and behavior. But fighting never brings about a real change in attitude. You cannot browbeat anyone into your own image and likeness. The key is humble love. Its power is such that it can do what fighting cannot: change both of you.

Another case is the one in which disdain or arrogance takes the fore. You're "listening" and you think to yourself, "I've heard that story a hundred times." You tune out, and there goes your dialogue. *Try gentleness.* The person you love is trying to express something you may never have *really* heard one hundred times previously. Listen gently to hear what you usually block out.

HAVE CONFIDENCE

Confidence...in the power of one's own words, but also
in the good will of both parties to the dialogue. Hence
dialogue promotes intimacy and friendship...and thus
excludes all self-seeking (83).

Confidence—this is the crux. You must have enough confidence to reveal the real you—not the self you think you would like to be or the self you think your spouse would like you to be. You must be confident your spouse will love the self you reveal even more than the you he or she already knew.

You must have confidence in your spouse—confidence that he or she is ready to accept you with real understanding. You must be confident like an innocent child who knows she is loved, like an infant who is perfectly confident he will not be dropped or injured.

You must let go, to stop clinging to that part of you that fears hurt and rejection, to put yourself, vulnerable, in your spouse's hands.

Lack of confidence is like an invisible wall. As long as it's there, you can see each other but cannot make real contact. You help each other lower the wall by saying "I love you" and revealing the deep feelings packed into those words.

USE GOOD JUDGMENT

The [speaker must]...learn the sensitivities of [the] audience, and if reason demands it, [the speaker] adapts himself and...his presentation to the susceptibilities and the degree of intelligence of his hearers (81.4).

Dialogue becomes unfruitful if negative feelings are allowed to take control. Good dialogue calls for good judgment. If you know or suspect that certain words will hurt your spouse, don't say them.

It can be helpful to reveal negative feelings about specific incidents, but only if you express your feeling instead of shifting the focus to your spouse. It can be helpful to say something like, "I felt frustrated and discouraged when you didn't call me at five o'clock." But it never helps to say, "Why didn't you call me at five o'clock like we agreed?" Once you criticize, the invisible wall

25

goes up and contact is lost. Put the emphasis on your feeling, not on what your spouse said or did.

When it comes to good memories, go back as far as you want. But leave bad memories alone. Do not go past yesterday when it comes to anything unpleasant that took place between you. (Certain therapeutic processes focus on bad memories. The dialogue described here is something else entirely.) The focus of dialogue is you and me, here and now: how I feel about myself, you, and us at this moment. If you maintain this focus with the attitudes recommended by Pope Paul, your dialogue will be rewarding.

LISTEN BEFORE SPEAKING

Before speaking,...listen...to what [they] say [and]...to what...[is] in their hearts (87).

Heart—that's the basis of true dialogue. *Listening* means being conscious of a person's feelings as well as words.

To listen to the total person, you need total attention. You must clear your mind of past and future—what happened an hour ago, what you are going to do an hour from now.

Before speaking, listen. Be careful to pay attention to what your spouse is saying now instead of thinking about what you want to say next. Pay attention to everything about your spouse. Look at him or her. Be physically close to heighten your sense of presence—not half a room apart or across the table from each other. Notice your spouse's eyes and facial expressions; they can reveal as much as words can. Notice your spouse's body position, hands, and feet.

Pay attention especially to your spouse's tone of voice. Words tell you ideas; the tone of voice lets you in on a whole world of feeling. Feelings are like a window on the person's inner world.

Your spouse's tone of voice can reveal that world to you. On the surface, words can be telling you a set of ideas. But on a deeper level, your spouse's voice can be telling you much more.

Listening is anything but a passive experience. It takes concentration to focus on a person. This total attention is a message in itself, telling your spouse, "I really care about you. I'm trying. I want to receive everything you want to give me at this moment." This message closes the gap between couples and allows the person speaking to trust and reveal. Listening is an act of love that creates relationship.

Families that change because of divorce, estrangement, or addiction require increased efforts in communication. The delicate fibers once knit into the original idea of family have been broken, frayed, and reknit into a new form. When a single parent, grandparent, other relative, or adult finds himself or herself the defined family head, communication with those no longer present is even more important. The words of Pope Paul VI on communication are even more valuable as a new family unit pushes into areas fraught with anger, resentment, violence, depression, and abuse.

Further Suggestions for Dialogue

The suggestions offered in this chapter pertain to all serious verbal communication between you and your spouse. But *dialogue,* practiced regularly, is a special activity in its own right. Couples who "dialogue" set aside certain times for it and go about it in a certain way.

Some couples dialogue every day, others less often. If you take up the practice—and you can only gain by doing so—you need to schedule it. If you dialogue only when you feel like it, you soon end up not doing it. Without a commitment to genuine dialogue, "more important things" always win out. Few couples would disagree with the idea of spending two hours a week in dialogue. After all, of the 168 hours in a week, two hours constitute one eighty-fourth of that time—not much to devote to something as important as your relationship. But very few couples spend even a half hour a week deliberately trying to communicate. It comes down to real priorities. You can recite a list of your so-called priorities. But does the way you spend your time match your theory?

Method and Topics

Many couples have found writing to be their key to fruitful dialogue. They begin by writing each other a letter on a topic of their choosing. After writing for ten minutes, each reads the other's letter. Then for another ten minutes they share the contents aloud.

This "love letter" approach has a number of benefits. One is that it allows clarity, which Pope Paul recommended. For a couple just beginning to dialogue, writing helps break the ice. Thinking and writing the words before speaking them makes it easier to verbally express sentiments you might otherwise feel hesitant or embarrassed to express. Those who dismiss this writing approach without ever trying it don't know what they're missing. Couples who practice this technique treasure their letters because they contain the words every spouse needs and wants to hear.

Some couples formulate their topics in the form of questions about feelings. For example: How do I feel when you pay me a compliment? (or when you get upset with me? when you are feeling "up"? when you are feeling "down"?) This area—how we influence each other's feelings—is uncharted territory for many couples. (For more on feelings, go to the end of this section for a list of words that express feelings.)

Almost anything about your life can be the focus of dialogue.

But some areas are deeper than others. If you've become used to sharing in this way, you can get into areas most couples never venture into, such as possessions, sex, death, or God. It's easy to look at those words on a page, but revealing your personal feelings about them to each other—that takes courage and trust. Try it and see.

As a couple, you have the awesome power to deepen each other's ability to love and to accept love. This deepening takes place when you truly communicate. You release God's creative love, which allows you and then others to experience the banquet that has already begun. The kingdom of God is in the midst of you. That is most evident when you are in dialogue.

Words That Express Feelings

The kind of dialogue recommended here embodies the wisdom of Jesus, expressed in Matthew 7:1—"Do not judge." But avoiding judgments in personal dialogue is not easy. One way to avoid judging is to leave unsaid any sentence in which the word *that* could follow *I feel.* For example, "I feel that it's too early" expresses a judgment, not a feeling. "I feel comfortable (sad, confused, relaxed)" expresses a feeling. When you write or say *I feel* in dialogue, follow it with a feeling word.

Use the following list to start a list of your own. Add other words that express other feelings you sometimes have.

affectionate	ashamed	calm
afraid	beaten	carefree
aggressive	belligerent	cautious
airy	bewildered	choked-up
alarmed	bored	close
angry	breathless	comforted
anxious	burdened	compassionate
appealing	bushed	confident

confused	gutless	respectful
contemptuous	happy	sad
contented	hard	scared
cooperative	hopeful	seductive
courageous	hopeless	self-assured
dead-eyed	horrified	sexy
deferential	humble	silly
defiant	immobilized	soft
dependent	impatient	spineless
depressed	inadequate	stretched
determined	independent	strong
dishonest	insecure	submissive
distant	irritated	sunshiny
dominant	itchy	surprised
dull	jealous	sweaty
ecstatic	joyful	sympathetic
edgy	light	talkative
embarrassed	locked-in	taut
empathetic	lonely	tender
enraged	loving	tense
envious	mixed-up	terrified
estranged	nauseated	thankful
evasive	open	threatened
excited	panicky	thrilled
fearful	paralyzed	timid
firm	peaceful	tolerant
frisky	played out	torn
frustrated	pleased	two-faced
giddy	powerless	uptight
grateful	proud	vacant
grief-stricken	quiet	warm
grumpy	relaxed	weepy
guilty	resentful	

Points for Reflection and Dialogue

This chapter is for the adults in the family. Go through the dialogue points together—because that's how you really experience what this chapter is about. One of the main reasons some families are not closer is that they don't realize how close they already are.

The best way to work through the points is to take one point a day on consecutive days to write and read each other's answer, and then talking. Pick a time and a place, then try it. If you've never done this kind of thing before, be ready for a surprise. Once you take the plunge, you'll understand much better what "the kingdom among you" can mean to you.

1. When I think back on all you've done for me, the one thing that stands out in my mind is... (Tell what it is and the feeling this memory brings. Write for at least five minutes, but not more than ten.)
2. When I realize some people go twenty-five or more years loving each other without really expressing it in a way that lights up their lives, I want to say to you...
3. When I say "I love you," part of what I mean is...
4. When I talk to you and sense that you're really trying to understand me, the feeling I have about you is...
5. When I remember you love me just as I am, the feelings I have about myself and about you are...
6. When you look into my eyes, the feeling that comes to me is...
7. When you're trying to tell me how you feel and I realize I am failing you by talking about facts or the way things are objectively, the feelings I have about myself and about you are...
8. Though I know you better than anybody else, there's so much about you I don't know. Recently I realized this when...

9. When we go through our wedding album, the main feeling that comes to me is… (Optional: Select your favorite pictures and write about them one at a time, a day at a time.)

10. Someone wrote, "To say 'I love you' is to say 'You will never die.' " What this means to me about you is…

4

Spouses Are Called
to Express Their Intimacy

(*CCC* 2360–2372)

The Intimate Garden

In the Book of Genesis, the story of Adam and Eve takes place in a garden. Estranged from God and from the garden he gave them, the man and the woman now have only each other. Whatever garden they experience from now on must come from their life together.

Most husbands and wives can appreciate the story. The world you live in is hardly a garden. Having become "one flesh," you toil together not only for bread, but for happiness. You have each other, and you know deep down that the only real garden in your lives is the one you live in together. The years come and go. Children come into your lives and one day leave for gardens of their own. What is left is the core of your world: God and each other, and finally, God.

Your garden of intimacy is the heart of your life together, and at the center of that garden is your experience of being "one flesh." The value of that experience cannot be overstated, because when it is an expression of personal love, it creates deeper love. As Pope Paul VI said in the Vatican II document Pastoral Constitution on the Church in the Modern World (*Gaudium et Spes*), "Married love is uniquely expressed and perfected by the exercise of the acts proper to marriage" (49).

Communication Is the Secret

Your sexual life together can deepen your personal intimacy. But impersonal sexual expression does not deepen a marriage. To be deepened by sex, *personal intimacy must already be present.*

There are two secrets to making sex an expression of personal intimacy. The first is to remember that *everything* about your relationship as a couple influences your sexual communication. The waking hours before sexual communication need to be a time of personal communication. If they aren't, there is need—*before* sex—for personal dialogue. Closeness begets closeness. Noncommunication begets no sex, impersonal sex, or sex that doesn't communicate the underlying love you have for each other.

The second secret involves the time right before, during, and after sexual love. The secret is to express yourself in ways your spouse understands and appreciates, to share yourself with all the trust and tenderness you have at a given moment, and to strive for the same qualities of gentleness, trust, prudence, and attention to each other that make true dialogue. The heart of the secret, in fact, is actual dialogue. Without loving verbal communication, your bodily communication lacks the fullness of personal intimacy it could have. When it comes to the human, spiritual, sacramental depths of sexual love, personal communication can make all the difference.

In his book *Seven Steps Toward Healing Your Marriage* (Liguori Publications, 2007), psychotherapist and marriage counselor William E. Rabior describes a real lover in marriage as having "deep generosity and concern for the beloved." When real lovers think of making love, their intent for unity "is almost Godlike in its scope." The willingness to be sensitive to the other's needs stretches into all waking hours and allows their love to flow naturally into sexual communication.

Sexual Myths and Real Problems

Sexuality is a deep part of the human mystery—so deep that every civilization has used sexual images and myths to express the mystery. But some very shallow sexual myths also exist. When people buy these myths, sex is dehumanized and personal relationships are destroyed.

One such myth is that you should "perform"—and achieve sexual "success"—by following certain patterns. The popular press may lead people to believe they must have trim, youthful bodies and perform like superstars to experience deep, abiding sexual intimacy. Rabior warns couples of society's "fascination with anything sexual," especially with regard to personal sexual satisfaction, and focus on an almost "explosive" sexual experience. The temptation to compare one's personal situation to that of others or to the standards made up by the latest sex oracles destroys the unique spirit of the marital relationship.

In their book *9 Ways to Nurture Your Marriage* (Liguori Publications, 2000), Rabior and his wife, Susan C. Rabior, advise that the gift of married life includes "the sheer physical pleasure that sex can bring" because a marital relationship is "the best and most appropriate place for full sexual expression, not just because of its procreative possibilities but because a sexual relationship belongs exclusively within the joys of a committed relationship." Every marriage is as unique as the individuals. No one pattern of sexual activity applies to all husbands and wives. There is no scorecard to keep regarding frequency of sex—how many times per week or month, no clock for how long foreplay should last, no rules of order for bodily positions or for what times of day or night sex should take place.

Sex is a personal expression, and every couple is unique. Unless it is free of fanciful goals, quotas, and expectations, sex cannot be an expression of personal intimacy.

Another myth about sex is that it's simply a means to private satisfaction. Pleasure is an integral part of sexual satisfaction, but the pleasure of sex is paradoxic. If you seek pleasure as pleasure, it will be fleeting. If you seek pleasure to express love, to achieve deeper oneness, it satisfies in a way that is abiding.

In your intimate garden, you are one flesh, one body. Your sexual intimacy—a basic expression of matrimony, your personal sacrament—sustains and deepens your family oneness in Jesus Christ.

Sexual Problems Need Communication

It's not uncommon for husbands and wives to have physical problems related to sex. Two common problems of men, for example, are secondary impotence (inability to sustain an erection sufficient for penetration) and premature ejaculation. Two common problems of women are lack of sexual desire and inability to have an orgasm.

These problems have various causes. According to psychotherapist William Rabior in *Seven Steps,* "Much sexual dysfunction is caused not by psychological factors as used to be thought, but by physical ones. Adding some medications, such as those for erectile dysfunction, or changing medications that inhibit sexual desire can help a great deal. Consult with your physician and your pharmacist. Some couples may also benefit from sex therapy with a competent sex therapist."

Stress or declining health, for example, can cause secondary impotence. Fear of failing to perform well or the husband's lack of sensitivity can also inhibit sexual desire and orgasm in women.

There are many ways to ease such problems, but one sure way to prolong or aggravate them is to ignore them, carry unexpressed bad feelings about them, or express resentment or hostility. What is needed and called for is *dialogue*—open, trust-filled communication. This is no time to fight or bury feelings; it is a time for love. Without *personal* intimacy in such instances, there will be no *physical* intimacy.

Getting help in such cases amounts to an act of love for Christ and his body, because a problem in the area of physical intimacy can affect personal intimacy—and that affects us all.

Good News for Intimacy: Natural Family Planning

In the late 1960s, millions of adult Catholics read Pope Paul VI's Encyclical Letter on the Regulation of Births (*Humanae Vitae*), the 1968 document that rejected artificial forms of birth control. A major contribution to vision outlined in the encyclical is scientific advancement in natural family planning (NFP).

Around the world, a groundswell of interest in NFP has arisen on the part of young women who fear the Pill and other artificial means of birth control. Disenchantment with artificial means coincides with the spread of research-perfected NFP, which is safe, reliable, harmless, and costs absolutely nothing.

NFP is much more than a natural answer to artificial birth control. One of the most striking values married couples experience through NFP is a noticeable improvement in their family life. As they check the monthly cycle and make decisions *together*, couples report a new dimension in their communication as spouses. A heightening of communication and sexual interest go together. After switching from artificial means, wives commonly say things like, "Now my husband asks me again, and doesn't take me for granted any more." From their husbands we hear, "My wife is interested again; she reacts now like when we were first married."

It's a surprise to many that NFP makes people more aware of the kingdom of God among them. Because NFP helps husbands and wives share in an intimate dimension of human relationship, they experience increased confidence in one another, a heightened sense of trust, and a better understanding of God's presence in their marriage. This deeper union reflects the light of Christ's love and witnesses to the reality of God's kingdom on earth as in heaven. Many NFP couples admit to feeling a powerful sense of being in union with God's will in their marriage and family life.

The intimate garden you share as spouses is the place where you experience the kingdom of peace and joy in the Spirit. It is from this experience of "one flesh" that your married love goes out and gives life to the rest of Christ's body, beginning with your own family.

Points for Reflection and Dialogue

The material in this chapter will help you deepen your personal closeness and help you renew your sexual communication. So take the opportunity. Discover new areas of intimacy by answering these questions together.

1. When I think of us as "two in one flesh," working our way through life together, I think...
2. When I think of our marriage as an intimate garden that nobody lives in but you, me, and God, I realize...
3. The activity in our daily life together that helps me feel closest to you is...

4. The quality you show that does the most to make our love-making an experience of love is…(Describe how this quality influences your attitude and feelings.)
5. One way you can help me communicate better when we are making love is…
6. What I have heard or read until now about NFP is…
7. My reaction to NFP is…
8. When I realize you and I can always love each other more and more if we really want to, I…
9. When I realize our personal intimacy can give others a consciousness of Christ's loving presence in their lives, I…

5

YOU ARE CALLED TO
LISTEN AND PRAY TOGETHER

(*CCC* 2650–2719)

Listening Through Sacred Scripture

You live with people who need your listening heart. And you live with God, whose deep desire is that you listen to *his* heart. Here and now, God calls to you through the words of sacred Scripture. In the words of Pope Paul VI's 1965 Vatican II document Dogmatic Constitution on Divine Revelation (*Dei Verbum*), God invites you through "the fullness of his love…into his own company" (2). His great desire is that you listen to him in Scripture and respond to him in prayer. Pope Paul urged, "prayer should accompany the reading of sacred Scripture" (25).

Suggestions for Family Scripture

Until Vatican II, reading and praying the Scripture was a tradition of relatively few Catholic families. If your family has not made that experience a regular part of your life together, take the following suggestions. Even if Scripture is already part of your family tradition, these suggestions may contain a few helpful ideas for you too.

- **Read and pray Scripture together regularly.** How often and how long varies with each family. Once you've chosen the time, consider it sacred—a time when you deliberately want to be together to love one another by sharing the Word.
- **Choose the time carefully.** Young children's bedtime works well for a brief reading of a favorite Gospel passage. Other families prefer to read Scripture just before the main family meal; the meal prayer together can then be based on the Scripture passage. A longer session at least once a week is also a good idea; for many, Saturday or Sunday evening is an ideal time.
- **Allow prayer time to ease transitions.** If children live in two places or spend alternate weekends with another parent or family member, the return home is a good time to focus on prayer and Scripture to ritualize the moment and ease the transition back into the family home. Parents or adults waiting for the return of their absent children should resist the temptation to dive into the multitude of tasks that need to be done before the children return by immersing themselves in prayer.
- **Let the children do as much as possible.** Active involvement is the key to maintaining their interest. Every contribution they make should be appreciated, no matter how young they are. Do your best to make these get-togethers a joyful experience for the children. Their memories of these times will have a profound influence on their relationships with you, with each other, and with God.
- **Prayer should be part of family Scripture time.** After the reading and sharing of thoughts, each family member should have a chance to simply talk to Jesus or the Father or the Spirit. (If you're reading Saint Paul or one of the prophets, talk to them

too; they hear you.) Take turns talking in your own words. If the Spirit moves the group to pray in silence, that too is very good. Parents, during this prayer time, remember to express your own personal response to God, avoiding sermonettes aimed at the children.

A Format for Family Scripture

1. **Everyone should focus on the presence of Jesus among you.** "For where two or three are gathered in my name, I am there among them" (Matthew 18:20).
2. **A family member reads the chosen passage.** If you aren't following a Scripture-reading plan, let the reader choose the passage.
3. **After the reading, begin to digest it.** You can do this by taking either a study-oriented approach or a personal approach. In the *study-oriented approach*, look for the general sense of the passage as a whole as well as the meaning of the individual sentences. Use commentary, dictionaries, Bible atlas, footnotes, and the introduction of the Gospel, letter, or book to understand the passage's connection with the rest of the chapter or section it's part of. In the *personal approach,* everyone reflects on the passage for a minute or two, then spends about five minutes writing (or drawing) their thoughts and feelings about the reading. A focus question that works with most readings: "What did the Lord tell me in this reading that can make us a closer family?"
4. **Share.** Take turns telling or reading what each person wrote or drew or learned from research. After each has had a turn, invite general remarks about what was said and specific suggestions for future sessions. End with a family resolution— something positive all can do between now and next time.

5. **Do another planned activity.** Have a memorization contest, a Scripture game, or a snack.
6. **Pray together.**
7. **Share a sign of peace and joy.** Embrace, shake hands, kiss. Take your time; talk to each other personally. Express love, forgiveness, and joy in being together.

Listening Through Silent Prayer

Family prayer takes many forms. Various methods or techniques, such as the rosary, can be used together as well as privately. One thing to remember about any prayer technique is that it's good for you if it helps you be in touch with God—and not good for you if it doesn't. Another thing to remember: all prayer is supernatural in the sense that it's a response to God that begins with a grace from God. If your prayer is real, it's supernatural prayer regardless of the technique you use.

Centering Prayer

This method, the name of which was inspired by the Trappist monk and writer Thomas Merton, is a simplified form of the prayer in the fourteenth-century Catholic spiritual classic, *The Cloud of Unknowing.*

1. **Find a quiet place, sit in a comfortable position, and close your eyes.** Relax your muscles as completely as possible. Relax your mind, breathe deeply, and enjoy the inner calm.
2. **For several moments focus calmly on the presence of God—Father, Son, and Spirit—at the center of your being.** God is the center who is everywhere, present at the deep center of your soul. Focus on that center. Allow yourself to experience God present within it.

3. **Let a word come to you—a simple word like God, Father, Love, Jesus, Lord, or Yahweh.** Slowly and calmly repeat the word. Let it lead you into God present at your center. Focus all your attention and desire on God, and let your word express all the faith, hope, love, and praise within you. If any thoughts or interruptions cause you to lose your focus, simply return to the center by repeating your word.

4. **End your prayer slowly and calmly.** Slowly repeat a prayer such as the Our Father, the Hail Mary, or the Glory Be, experiencing all that the words bring to you.

For private centering prayer, take about 20 minutes at least once (if possible, twice) a day. For family prayer, shorten the time for younger children. In shortened form it can be used as silent prayer in your family Scripture get-togethers.

In your relationship with God through Scripture and listening, there is what the eminent theologian Bernard Lonergan has called the *outer word* and the *inner word.* The *outer word* is meaning that comes to you from understanding Scripture itself. *Inner word* is the word God speaks to your heart, the word Jesus was talking about when he said, "Blessed are you, Simon son of Jonah! For flesh and blood has not revealed this to you, but my Father in heaven" (Matthew 16:17).

Receiving this inner word is not something you can make happen. It is grace, an experience of the kingdom among you. But you can prepare for it by listening faithfully. Hearing the inner word is something like hearing what someone's heart is saying *through* the words he or she says to you. The inner word comes from God's heart to yours.

Saint Augustine said poignantly, "Our hearts are restless until they rest in you." When you listen to God and to each other with enough love, your hearts become full.

Points for Reflection and Dialogue

1. When I think God wants me, is inviting me, to be intimate with him, I...

2. I want to make Scripture a more regular part of my life because...

3. The day and time we've agreed to read Scripture together is...

4. The Scripture passage we'll read next time is...

5. The main blessing I think we received from our last Scripture get-together was...

6. Silent prayer helps me to be in touch with God because...

7. The greatest gift I've received from listening to God in Scripture is...

8. The greatest gift I've received from listening to my family sharing their experience of God is...

6

YOU ARE CALLED TO FAMILY FORGIVENESS

(CCC 2838–2845)

A Way of Family Forgiveness

I am Jesus whom you are persecuting...persecuting...PERSECUT-ING. Why do you persecute me...me...ME? (see Acts 22:7).

Those words echoed in the memory of Paul until the day he died. As the years went on, their meaning became clearer and clearer, until Paul could declare, "If one member suffers, all suffer together with it; if one member is honored, all rejoice together with it" (1 Corinthians 12:26).

As a family with Jesus among you, you are called to reconcile when you cause each other suffering. You are called to share his forgiveness. Coming together and being healed by that forgiveness is one of the most amazing graces you possess. The more you use this grace, the more you experience the presence and love of Christ in your family.

Focus on Family Relationships

The following list contains positive and negative aspects of family life. The left column consists of positive elements that strengthen your family body by deepening your closeness and joy. The right column consists of negative elements that weaken your family body by causing suffering and alienation.

Use the list as is or (and this may be a better idea) to make up your own list—one that contains more of the positive and negative things that pertain to your family's experiences. You may want to have two lists: one for adults and teenagers and a second, simpler one for children.

In using your list, balance positive and negative. If you use only the negative points, you might get the impression you don't love your family very much, which isn't true—you're much more loving than unloving. If you find it easier to spot negative elements in your own conduct, it's because you're not as loving toward yourself as you could be.

Go down both columns, focusing on your relationships within the family by writing (or thinking of) one person's name in each box you select. Be selective; zero in on the ones that apply to you and skip the rest. One set of points might look like this:

SHARING versus SELFISHNESS	
I shared with...	**I was selfish to...**
_____ by being generous with my time.	_____ by being stingy with my time.

After coming together and centering on the presence of Jesus among you, pray for a spirit of love and forgiveness. Then, silently together, go down your list(s) point by point. At the end of the list are suggestions on what to do next.

SHARING versus SELFISHNESS

I shared with...	I was selfish to...
_____ by being generous with my time.	_____ by being stingy with my time.
_____ by volunteering to help out.	_____ by avoiding a chance to help out.
_____ by being generous with my clothes, toys, equipment.	_____ by being selfish with my clothes, toys, equipment.
_____ by gladly doing it his/her way.	_____ by insisting it be done my way.
_____ by saying, "Sure, I can spare the time."	_____ by saying "Sorry, I haven't got the time."
_____ by saying, "Let's do it together."	_____ by saying, "It's your job, your turn."
_____ by saying, "Let's try it your way."	_____ by saying, "Don't do it that way."

CARING versus INDIFFERENCE

I cared about...	I was indifferent to...
_____ by listening when...	_____ by not listening when...
_____ by asking how he/she felt about...	_____ by not caring how he/she felt about...
_____ by taking him/her seriously about...	_____ by making fun of him/her.
_____ by asking...	_____ by demanding...

RESPECT versus DISRESPECT	
I respected...	**I disrespected...**
_____ by caring whether I would hurt his/her feelings when...	_____ by not caring whether I would hurt his/her feelings when...
_____ by asking whether I had hurt his/her feelings when...	_____ by not asking whether I had hurt his/her feelings when...
_____ by giving full attention to him/her when...	_____ by pretending to be busy when...
_____ by dropping what I was doing when...	_____ by complaining when...
_____ by...	_____ by...

PRAISE versus CRITICISM	
I praised...	**I criticized...**
_____ for doing...	_____ for doing...
_____ for remembering to...	_____ for forgetting to...
_____ for looking nice.	_____ for the way he/she looked.
_____ for the way he/she...	_____ for the way he/she...
_____ by saying, "Thanks for..."	_____ by saying, "It's about time."
_____ by saying, "You're good at..."	_____ by saying, "You never..."
_____ by saying something gentle when I was upset.	_____ by saying, "Shut up!"
_____ by calling him/her a nickname he/she likes.	_____ by calling him/her a name he/she doesn't like.
_____ by saying...	_____ by saying...
_____ by saying...	_____ by saying...

TRUST versus SUSPICION

I trusted...	I was suspicious of...
_____ and showed it when...	_____ by thinking I couldn't trust him/her when...
_____ by believing he/she would tell me when...	_____ by trying to worm information out of him/her when...
_____ by thinking of a good reason he/she had for doing...	_____ by thinking he/she was trying to make me feel bad when...
_____ by taking his/her word for it when...	_____ by suspecting he/she lied to me when...
_____ by thinking, "Maybe the mistake was mine."	_____ by saying, "It's *your* fault."
_____ by presuming he/she was doing something good.	_____ by saying, "What are you doing *now*?"

UNDERSTANDING versus CONTROL

I tried to understand...	I tried to control...
_____ by treating him/her the way I'd like to be treated when...	_____ by being bossy when...
_____ by realizing he/she has feelings like mine.	_____ by making threats when...
_____ by realizing he/she deserves my deepest respect.	_____ by nagging and picking at him/her about...
_____ by letting him/her be when there is no harm in it.	_____ by frequently saying *no*.
_____ by laying conditions on him/her only when necessary.	_____ by saying *unless* or *or else*.
_____ by going along with him/her when...	_____ by saying, "Why *should* I?"

MAKING PEACE versus FIGHTING

I made peace with...	I fought with...
_____ by saying, "I love you."	_____ by teasing him/her about...
_____ by saying, "Let's be friends and talk."	_____ by starting an argument about...
_____ by refusing to push, shove, hit, or slap when...	_____ by pushing, shoving, hitting, or slapping him/her when...
_____ by expressing my feelings when...	_____ by deliberately doing... to annoy him/her.
_____ by asking forgiveness when...	_____ by accusing him/her of...
_____ by following my rule never to hurt a family member.	_____ by insulting him/her or being sarcastic when...

FORGIVENESS versus HOSTILITY

I was forgiving toward...	I was hostile toward...
_____ by sacrificing my pride and making the first move when...	_____ by maintaining a "cold war" with him/her when...
_____ by saying, "Let's be friends" when...	_____ by acting aloof when...
_____ by touching him/her gently when...	_____ by slamming the door or breaking something when...
_____ by saying sincerely, "That's OK; I know you didn't mean it" when...	_____ by getting upset with him/her when...
_____ by saying, "I'm really sorry; please forgive me" when...	_____ by refusing to approach him/her after I had hurt him/her by...
_____ by saying, "You're right; let's make up" when...	_____ by refusing to accept his/her attempt to reconcile with me when...

Each person should silently go over his or her list, then go back over the positive points. Thank God for the love you all have been given—this is evidence of his loving presence in your own being.

Have each person silently go over the negative points on his/her list. Ask for forgiveness and for help in asking forgiveness of someone whose name is noted after one of the negative points.

Join hands and pray the Our Father together. Each family member should go to the person he/she needs forgiveness from. Simply say something like, "Gerald, I was selfish when I told you I didn't have time to pick up your coat at the cleaner's. Please forgive me." After that, embrace, shake hands, or give some other sign of friendship.

After each family member has asked and given forgiveness, join together again and say a final prayer.

Toward the Sacrament of Reconciliation

The method of family forgiveness outlined above can be done in a ten-minute get-together. It can also be part of a longer family Scripture or prayer session (see chapter 5).

Family forgiveness is not the sacrament of penance and is in no way a substitute for it, but the two go together in a beautiful way. In family forgiveness, you experience the love of Christ, the healing of his body, and your own family as Church. In the sacrament of penance, you experience Christ's sure sign of forgiveness—absolution of your sins—and your deep oneness with the whole body of Catholics in whom he lives.

Points for Reflection and Dialogue

1. "If one member suffers, all suffer together." What this means to me when I think of my family is...
2. The way I am most sharing in our family is...
3. The way I want to be more sharing is...
4. The main way I take away from the peace of Christ in our family is by...
5. The way I intend to deepen the peace of Christ in our family is by...
6. The greatest gift I've received from family reconciliation is...

7

YOU ARE CALLED TO EXPERIENCE THE EUCHARIST

(*CCC* 1324–1405)

The Eucharist, Center of Family Life

A most fascinating yet basic symbol in nature is the *mandala*, a circular design that radiates outward from a point at the center. The flat top of a tree stump is a perfect mandala—rings growing outward from a central point of life. Nature produces mandalas, such as flowers opening out, in wild generosity. Artists use the design to express what words and even music cannot say.

The meanings found in the mandala are as varied as its forms. Through the ages it has symbolized wholeness, organic oneness, healing, and growth, all finding their source in the life-giving center.

For Catholics, the great mandala of Christian life always has been, and always will be, Jesus Christ in the Eucharist. He is, as Pope John Paul II said in his 1979 encyclical *Redemptor Hominis,* "the center of the universe and of history" (1). As Saint Paul discovered on the road outside Damascus, Christ is not limited by what we call space and time—his presence envelops and passes through the space-time continuum. And yet we can know him "in the breaking of the bread" (Luke 24:35). In that act of nourishment, we experience the living center of our existence—uniting us, his body, ever more closely to the source of life that has no limits.

Center of Meaning

Your life is organized in all kinds of ways. And yet, despite all the programming of human life, you may know the feeling many people express—that their lives have no real center. All the activity, the competition, the getting ahead—it all seems to lead nowhere. At the deep level where we all really live, these people experience their center as a void, an empty place that sends this silent message: Your life is a senseless trip in a mindless universe, ending in oblivion.

Certainly, many people are not afflicted with that disease. Among them are Catholics who have never lost, or who have recovered, the center of their lives—that living Bread who nourishes his body with meaning and unity.

The key to your meaning and oneness as a family is to deepen or recover your center. Every day you work, play, study, eat, and sleep in what can be an endless round of mere functions, a series of meaningless movements. But it doesn't have to be that way. You can focus on the center and let your life together flow toward and out from it. You can consciously let that center tie the scattered remnants of your days into one meaningful reality of never-ending value. You can focus on the Eucharist with such steady consciousness that it becomes your "still point," the silent source of life that lets your family realize the depth of Paul's words: "Because there is one bread, we who are many are one body, for we all partake of the one bread" (1 Corinthians 10:17).

Focus of Family Meals

At home, one of the most valuable ways of focusing on the Eucharist is to make it the center of attention at the start of family meals. Even in less-than-ideal circumstances, it's possible to lead off the meal with a moment of deep attention to Jesus Christ. This moment is part of the grace before the meal, but it needs to be a special moment—a brief, silent time for each person to focus on the living Bread.

Make this moment specifically Eucharistic: train your hearts on the Eucharist and realize your oneness with each other in him. If you each memorize the words of 1 Corinthians 10:17, "Because there is one bread, we who are many are one body, for we all partake of the one bread," and repeat them in your heart before every family meal, the eucharistic Presence will in time become the still point of your turning world.

Weekly Mass:
The Banquet of Family Oneness

The Eucharist is the "source and summit" of Christian life (*LG* 11). For this reason, Catholic families draw closer to one another at the living center of the eucharistic community. History shows how easy it is to lose vital contact with that center. As early as AD 57, one group of Christians had let the Eucharistic gathering degenerate into a time of excessive drinking, alienation, and hurt feelings. In 1 Corinthians 11:27, Paul brought that group back to reality by reminding them in no uncertain terms, "Whoever, therefore, eats the bread or drinks the cup of the Lord in an unworthy manner will be answerable for the body and blood of the Lord."

Loss of contact with the Eucharist today takes different forms, but the solution is the same. We can experience deeper meaning and joy in weekly Mass if we focus more deeply on Christ at the center of it all. Once the basic insight comes into focus—that "Christ is all and in all!" (Colossians 3:11)—everything else falls into perspective. The following suggestions may help your family grow together into this realization:

- **Bring an essential awareness of Jesus' passion, death, and resurrection to weekly Mass.** The Sunday Scripture readings, which are read at Saturday-evening Mass as well as at Sunday Mass, show a different side of the mystery of Christ; when taken together over a three-year period, they give the total picture. But at the very center of that picture is the unchanging core of what each Mass is all about: his passion, death, and resurrection. As you focus on the Sunday readings, it's essential not to lose sight of that vital center.
- **Link the Eucharist with your family Scripture sessions by basing them on the Sunday Mass readings.** Remembering your family session as you listen to the readings and homily at Mass will bring out the family/Church dimension of the Word you're hearing and help the homily reinforce your sense of family oneness.
- **Turn your mind to each member of your family during the preparation of gifts.** As a family, the main thing you offer to God in Jesus can be your sense of family oneness. You desire this oneness, and you work to discover the kingdom among you. Now is the time to offer your efforts and the graced experience of closeness that flow from those efforts. If you're sitting next to each other, give each other a look of recognition to remind yourselves of what you're offering. This alone is a key reason to be together as a family, whenever possible, at weekly Mass.
- **Focus on Jesus during the eucharistic prayer (after the preface up to the Lord's Prayer).** Jesus is with you here and

now, reenacting his passion, death, and resurrection. Keep this focus, letting the words of the eucharistic prayer lend meaning to it. When the priest says "Do this in memory of me" at the heart of the eucharistic prayer, let your vision of the Last Supper be as vivid as possible.

- **Take a moment to find special meaning in the sign of peace for you as a family.** It doesn't have to be anything showy; a look and a touch can say a great deal.
- **Focus on the depth of holy Communion.** Granted, holy Communion possesses such meaning that the reality of it cannot be fathomed by the human mind, but one way to prepare yourself to receive Communion is to repeat to yourself the fourteenth-century prayer *Anima Christi*:

> *Soul of Christ, sanctify me;*
> *Body of Christ, save me;*
> *Blood of Christ, inebriate me;*
> *Water of Christ's side, wash away my sins;*
> *Passion of Christ, comfort me;*
> *O sweet Jesus, listen to me;*
> *In Thy wounds I fain would hide;*
> *Ne'er to be parted from Thy side;*
> *Guard me, should the foe assail me;*
> *Call me when my life will fail me;*
> *Bid me come to Thee above;*
> *With Thy saints to sing Thy love;*
> *World without end; Amen.*

Saint Augustine wrote that when the priest offers you the body of Christ, you should reply *Amen,* meaning "So be it!" And by this reply we consent to become the body of Christ. *We* means the threefold body of Christ: his risen body, his body the Church, and his eucharistic body. When you say *Amen*, you are saying "Yes, we are the body of Christ."

Recall the words of Paul you repeat to yourself before meals: "Because there is one bread, we who are many are one body, for we all partake of the one bread" (1 Corinthians 10:17). As the mysterious reality of Jesus' death becomes present here and now, so does the future of your family's life together in the kingdom. The future banquet is now. Pray for the fullness of love for Christ within you, love for his body—especially your family—with whom you are now more one than ever before. With Jesus, you and your family are now, as Augustine said, "one Christ, loving himself."

Points for Reflection and Dialogue

1. The Emmaus story in Luke 24:13–35 tells me this about the Eucharist: …
2. Since I started repeating 1 Corinthians 10:17 silently before family meals, I have begun to realize…
3. When I try to probe the meaning of "Christ is all, and in all!" (Colossians 3:11), the main thought or feeling that comes to me is…
4. The main realization that comes to me when I offer our gift of family oneness during the preparation of gifts is…
5. What the eucharistic prayer at weekly Mass has meant to me since I began to focus on it more deeply is…
6. What the sign of peace has come to mean to me as a family sign is…
7. Now that I receive holy Communion as the banquet of our family oneness, the thoughts and feelings I have about Communion are…(Write as much as you can on this point.)

8

YOU ARE CALLED
TO EVANGELIZE

(CCC 2373–2386)

Your Family's Essential Function

If you were a first-century Christian trying to write an orderly account of the movement sparked by Jesus of Nazareth, how would you organize your material? This was one of the literary problems Luke the Evangelist had to work out.

We can trace Luke's method by studying his two-part masterpiece—his Gospel and The Acts of the Apostles. Luke's Gospel narrative is cast in the form of a journey toward Jerusalem, where Jesus has an appointment with death and resurrection (9—18). Picking up the narrative after the resurrection, Acts records the astounding growth of the Christian movement as it journeyed outward from Jerusalem "to the ends of the earth" (1:8).

This image—a community growing outward from its center, the risen Jesus—is Luke's inspired way of delivering his Gospel message to your family. His message: You are Jesus' witnesses to the world. Your calling as a family is to be his body in such a way that people sense this vital fact: *Jesus lives!*

In his 1975 apostolic exhortation Evangelization in the Modern World (*Evangelii Nuntiandi*), Pope Paul VI declared evangelization to be the "essential function" (14) of the Church; therefore, it is also the essential function of your family (71). Your oneness in love as a family is the "silent witness" (21) living "a life truly and essentially Christian," (41) which leads people to raise "a spirit of inquiry" (21) about the Church and about Christ himself.

Evangelization Begins at Home

But how does a family become so "truly and essentially Christian" that other people experience Jesus through that family? The Pope's answer: "The Church begins her work of evangelization by evangelizing herself" (*EN* 15). In other words, evangelization begins at home.

Begin in our own homes. Make them centers of compassion. Forgive endlessly. This is how we journey to our center as in Luke's Gospel. Then comes the next part of evangelization— journeying outward from the center to "the ends of the earth," as in Acts of the Apostles.

But what does all this mean in the real world we live in? Society is shaped by economic and political systems that often seem to do more harm than good in a world filled with pain, bloodshed, loneliness, and death. How can one family, or a group of families, be Christ-bearers in such a situation?

You will find the answer if you reflect on the following questions *together*. Everyone has something to offer, no matter how large or small. Make a plan *together*, a plan that allows each family member to live the Christian faith and be a *visible* sign of Christ's love in the world.

CELEBRATING OUR FAITH

- One day we will be together sharing God who is love, goodness, truth, and bliss. How will we deepen our sense of this eternal adventure and delight as we worship together each week?
- How will we make our weekends together times of greater joy to remind us of our eternal future?

INFLUENCING POPULAR MEDIA

- How will our family "send a message" to those in the media, entertainment field, World Wide Web enterprises, and publishers whose products tear down human life?
- How will we affirm the ones who are doing *good* work?
- How will we react to trashy television shows in our own home?

RESPECTING HUMAN LIFE

- How will we show we are as serious about protecting the lives of the unborn as we are about protecting future generations from nuclear holocaust?
- How will we show that—as the Vatican has documented—the arms race "kills the poor by causing them to starve"?
- How will we react to the use of nicotine, alcohol, and other drugs to show we respect our own lives and health?

BEING GOOD STEWARDS OF THE EARTH

- How will we influence corporations and governments to restore the earth and protect it for future generations?
- How will we make our property and vehicles as ecologically healthy as possible?